Quick Start Guides

LOWER CHOLESTEROL
DIET

A Quick Start
Guide
To
Lower Cholesterol

*Improve Your Health
and Feel Great!*

***PLUS* Over 100 Delicious Cholesterol Lowering Recipes**

First published in 2015 by Erin Rose Publishing

Text and illustration copyright © 2015 Erin Rose Publishing

Design: Julie Anson

ISBN: 978-0-9933204-0-8

A CIP record for this book is available from the British Library.

DISCLAIMER: This book is for informational purposes only and not intended as a substitute for the medical advice, diagnosis or treatment of a physician or qualified healthcare provider. The reader should consult a physician before undertaking a new health care regime and in all matters relating to his/her health, and particularly with respect to any symptoms that may require diagnosis or medical attention.

While every care has been taken in compiling the recipes for this book we cannot accept responsibility for any problems which arise as a result of preparing one of the recipes. The author and publisher disclaim responsibility for any adverse effects that may arise from the use or application of the recipes in this book. Some of the recipes in this book include nuts and eggs. If you have an egg or nut allergy it's important to avoid these. It is recommended that children, pregnant women, the elderly or anyone who has an immune system disorder avoid eating raw eggs.

CONTENTS

Recipes

Lunch 29

Dinner...69

INTRODUCTION

Thousands of people every year are diagnosed with high cholesterol which increases the risk of circulatory problems, heart disease and strokes. The likelihood is if you are reading this book that you or a family member is one of them. Or maybe you are at risk and want to prevent diseases linked with high cholesterol then this Quick Start Guide is for you! You can take charge of your own health and lower your cholesterol.

Things have changed dramatically in recent years and the previous advice is no longer valid. New research shows that many of the foods we were told to avoid do not have the negative impact on blood cholesterol after all. That will come as welcome news, especially if you were avoiding the foods you love and still have high cholesterol despite your best efforts.

There is a glut of products on the market aimed at reducing cholesterol yet everyday we are unwittingly eating foods which are raising our bad cholesterol so the problem isn't going away. Certain foods are best avoided completely. A healthy balanced diet is the way forward, once you know what that means. The really excellent news is there are delicious everyday foods which lower your cholesterol naturally so the cholesterol lowering diet is not so much about restriction but expanding your diet. By incorporating these beneficial foods into your diet you can lower your cholesterol and what's more, you can do it naturally.

In this book we bring you the essential information based on the newest findings in a comprehensive, easy to understand way, providing you with what you need to know to help you reduce your cholesterol, with plenty of tips plus plenty of delicious everyday recipes which mostly consist of store cupboard ingredients which are easy to source. You'll discover how you can make a positive impact on your future health by taking some simple straightforward steps. Whether you currently have high cholesterol, or are borderline, or even if you are concerned due to a family history of raised cholesterol or heart disease, it's never too soon to take action. If you are ready to make positive changes to you or your families health, read on!

What Is Cholesterol?

Cholesterol is a fatty substance (or lipid) which we all have, that ensures vital functions such as the healthy production of sex hormones, vitamin D, aids metabolic processes, digestion and cell function. We've heard about the good fats and the bad fats and when it comes to your cholesterol levels but what does that mean?

It boils down to this - LDL cholesterol (Low Density Lipoprotein) is the bad fat which causes accumulations of plaque deposits along the arteries which restricts the blood flow, a condition known as atherosclerosis which leads coronary heart disease. Then there is HDL (High Density Lipoprotein) which helps remove the bad fat deposits from the arteries carrying it back to the liver to be broken down before being eliminated by the body.

High levels of LDL cholesterol are linked with cardiovascular disease because the plaque deposits strain the heart causing it to work so much harder to pump blood around the body, plus it can split the arteries and cause blood clots to form. In turn the blood clots can cause strokes and heart attacks when the blood supply is interrupted.

What we eat plays a vital role in our cholesterol levels. Our body needs fats to function well, but the key is finding the balance between the good and bad fats. Not only do we get fats through our diet, the liver actually makes its own to meet the necessary requirements of the body. The body actually produces less cholesterol when we eat a little but produces more when you eat too little cholesterol.

There are no symptoms of high cholesterol. The only way to measure your cholesterol levels is to have a blood test to define both your LDL and HDL cholesterol.

What Causes High Cholesterol?

There are numerous factors which put you at risk of high cholesterol but YOU can do something about it. Making dietary changes is a huge step in the right direction and it's worth looking at where else improvements can be made to your everyday lifestyle.

Some of the risk factors which lead to high cholesterol and cardiovascular disease are:

- Diets high in trans-fats, sugars and carbohydrates and which are too low in fibre and healthy fats.
- Increasing age.
- Women who are post-menopausal.
- Existing health conditions; diabetes, kidney problems, pancreatitis and hypothyroid, high blood pressure.
- Obesity.
- Sedentary lifestyle.
- Smoking.
- Excessive alcohol consumption.
- Genetics; a family history of high cholesterol predisposes you to it, regardless of age.

High cholesterol (LDL) can sneak up on you, so it's worth getting tested to determine if you are at risk of sleep-walking into poor health. Once you know you can do something about it, you have the ability to turn it around and armed with basic but essential knowledge, you can learn how to improve your cholesterol levels and improve your own health. Check with your doctor before embarking on a change of diet to make sure it's safe for you to do so.

The Big Fat Mistake

Since the 1970's we were told saturated fat is bad for us. We were repeatedly told to avoid it, and despite our supermarket shelves exploding with low-fat products, levels of obesity, heart disease, high cholesterol and many other chronic diseases have rocketed. So if we're all eating less fat why is this?

The products we have been avoiding like steak, eggs, prawns, butter and cheese do not significantly raise cholesterol and the advice which has been dished out was unfounded. Eating these foods in moderation does not lead to high cholesterol, or prevent death from heart disease. New findings suggest that dairy fat in particular, is not a factor in cardiovascular disease and that it can actually lower the risk of obesity. Australian studies have shown that it lowers the risk of heart disease. However, like anything consumed in excessive quantities, it can lead to weight problems which raises the risk of heart disease - moderation is the key.

The saturated fat in the products we were warned not to eat because of the risk of developing dangerously high cholesterol is not the villain it had been portrayed to be! So if fat wasn't the problem, do we know what is?

Today, new evidence sheds light on sugar and excessive carbohydrate consumption as being the real culprit. One big plus point about fat is that it makes us feel satisfied and less likely to go looking for snacks to satisfy cravings after a meal, thus can help curb obesity. However, the same cannot be said for sugar!

Hidden Culprits In Our Everyday Foods

Sugar

Research shows that people who eat the most sugar have the highest blood triglyceride levels and lowest HDL (good cholesterol). Having low HDL cholesterol is a high risk factor for cardiovascular disease. A high sugar intake increases your risk of a heart attack.

The sweet deceit of this highly addictive, sneaky addition to masses of our everyday foods is that it triggers cravings for more sugar creating a cycle. Large peaks and troughs in blood sugar levels cause a need to sustain artificially stimulated energy levels. Sugar consumption leads to increased hunger and we're being unwittingly poisoned because it's being added to savoury foods. This harmful hidden additive can be hard to avoid with an everyday diet, and even more so if you consume fast foods. Reading the labels can be an eye-opener when you discover low-fat foods have sugar added to replace the fat which is creating an even greater problem. Even savoury foods like processed meats, marinated products and 'healthy' cereal bars can be loaded with sugar. Be aware when you go shopping. Check the labels.

> **Your maximum daily intake should be no more than 6-9 teaspoons of sugar a day, that's 24 – 36g.**

That may sound like a lot, especially if you aren't adding sugar to cereals or drinks, however reading food labels will show you just how sugar laden so many of our everyday products actually are.

Trans Fatty Acids – Hydrogenated Oils

Trans fatty acids, aka trans fatty acids, are considered doubly harmful because they not only raise LDL (bad cholesterol) but they lower HDL (good cholesterol). Trans fats are vegetable oils (may sound harmless but they're not), which have gone through an industrial process to add hydrogen, causing the oil to solidify at room temperature and extending the shelf-life of the oil. Hydrogenated fats have been linked with coronary disease, diabetes and obesity and they have infiltrated our ready-made products such as cakes, pastries, biscuits, crackers, tortilla chips and deep fried foods. Chemists have created margarines and low-fat spreads which have been marketed as healthy alternatives to butter. Always read the label for products containing hydrogenated oils.

Despite the bad press over saturated fat and especially butter, it does contain fatty acids which help to prevent weight gain, improve digestion and combat inflammation. It also contains Vitamin K2 which helps prevent cancer, osteoporosis and heart disease. When it comes down to the chemist versus the cow, many people instinctively opt for the more natural option. The bottom line is this natural product, especially if from grass feed cows, has important health benefits to prevent some of the most serious and prevalent diseases.

What Can I Eat? - The Foods To Avoid

To reduce your LDL cholesterol, steer clear of these foods:

- Hydrogenated and partially hydrogenated trans fats which are found in many processed foods such as margarines, pies, pastries, cakes and deep-fried products. Be vigilant when reading the labels of ready-made products.

- Processed meats such as sausages, burgers, bacon and ham have been associated with heart disease. It's thought that the nitrates they contain may be responsible, opt for fresh cuts of meat instead. Limit your intake of red meat to no more than twice a week.

- Reduce your intake of refined carbohydrates such as white bread and pasta which is low in fibre and a starchy carbohydrate. Opt for brown or wholemeal varieties which contain more fibre.

- Avoid or reduce foods containing sugar, in all its forms; refined sugar found in cakes, cookies, biscuits, sweets, sugary fizzy drinks, syrup and concentrated fruit juices where the fibre has been extracted.

Foods Which Improve Your Cholesterol

You can improve your cholesterol levels by daily eating more of the following:

- Nuts and seeds are a great form of protein, fibre and essential fatty acids so eat more pistachios, cashews, almonds, macadamias, brazils, walnuts, hazelnuts, pumpkin seeds, sunflower seeds and sesame seeds. Go for raw nuts which aren't salted or dry roasted.

- Eat more fibre in the form of vegetables, fruit and pulses. Not only are they a source of vitamins, minerals and antioxidants but the fibre helps combat cholesterol and its effects.

- Oats have been shown to actively lower LDL cholesterol so move them to the top of your daily menu! This is due to a fibre called beta-glucan which sticks to the cholesterol and helps to prevent it being absorbed into the bloodstream. Oats have been found to lower LDL cholesterol and boost HDL cholesterol so they are an all round winner. Porridge or oat based granola or muesli is a great way to start your day and oatcakes make a handy snack or addition to a lunch box.

- Olive oil and rapeseed oil helps raise HDL cholesterol. Add oils to salads or use garlic or herb infused oil as a dipping sauce. Avoid over-heating oils.

- Oily fish such as salmon, mackerel, sardines, trout and herring are a rich source of omega-3 fatty acids which is cholesterol lowering and reduces the risk of heart disease.

- Soya products eaten regularly have been shown to lower cholesterol possibly down to the isoflavones it contains. So eat more tofu, soya mince and soya milk.

Top Healthy Tips

Improving your diet is a huge step forward and for some of you it will require new adjustments to your everyday life and what you eat, so here are some tips to help make it easier and to maximise your health and well-being.

- Watch your consumption of starchy carbohydrates, especially white flour products.

- At mealtimes, you could try replacing carbohydrates with a heap of vegetables instead. This will cut down on your carbohydrate load and prevent you feeling too sluggish.

- Essential fatty acids are vital for the brain, skin, hormones and nerve function. It's not easy to over indulge on these rich fatty foods because your hunger will be satisfied pretty quickly. So instead of opting for a sugary snack, opt for a healthy fat option.

- Carry on-the-go snacks like nuts, seeds, cheese and olives for some quick sustenance.

- Reduce your salt intake.

- Eat your fruit with its fibre, so avoid pure orange juices where the fibre has been removed. It'll help reduce blood sugar spikes and help prevent the fruit sugar from being stored in the liver.

- Get plenty of exercise. It doesn't need to be strenuous but it does need to be regular. Get at least 30 minutes a day; walking, swimming and cycling are all beneficial.

- Green and white tea is high in antioxidants which help to breakdown fat in the blood. With that in mind you'll be pleased to hear that dark chocolate also has the same benefit, but make sure the chocolate is at least 70% cocoa which means it contains less sugar.

- Excessive alcohol can elevate cholesterol levels but a small intake of red wine can improve your good cholesterol.
- Quitting smoking is really important and while this may not be a walk in the park, there are options available to make it easier, ranging from nicotine replacement patches to acupuncture by a qualified practitioner.

Cravings

So let's not sugar coat this! If you've been eating what is classed today as a normal diet, you've probably been consuming too much sugar, and that's without adding it to cereals and hot drinks; it's difficult to avoid it. So with that in mind, you can expect some cravings. The strength of cravings can vary depending on what your usual sugar intake is. However, it won't take long to overcome it and your taste buds will adjust to new flavours.

Cleansing Your Body

Water can not only help cleanse and hydrate your body but it can also make you feel full which is great if you are trying to avoid tempting snacks in between meals. Drinking plenty of water is so good for you and it's widely accepted that 8 glasses a day is a healthy amount. To really flush out toxins from your body, drink water first thing in the morning, before you eat or drink anything else. Why not a coffee or a fruit juice? A large glass or two of cool water is best.

Large volumes of fluid leave the stomach and pass through to the intestines quicker than small volumes. Cool fluids empty more quickly too. A great way to start the day is to hydrate quickly first thing in the morning by enjoying a pint of cool water. You can add a squeeze of lemon or lime juice if you like. You'll not only feel refreshed but it'll carry away accumulated waste products. So, hydrate your body and you'll feel bright eyed, have clearer thoughts and it'll help banish early morning fatigue.

How To Read The Labels

To help you recognise when sugar and trans-fats have been added to food products, here is a list of what they are labelled on packaging as.

Sugar
Detailed on food labels as:

- Invert sugar syrup
- Cane juice crystals
- Dextrin
- Dextrose
- Glucose syrup
- Sucrose
- Fructose syrup
- Maltodextrin
- Barley malt
- Beet sugar
- Corn syrup
- Date sugar
- Palm sugar
- Malt syrup
- Dehydrated fruit juice
- Carob syrup
- Golden syrup
- Refiners syrup
- Ethylmaltol

Trans Fats
Detailed on food labels as:

- Hydrogenated vegetable oil
- Hydrogenated saturated fat
- Partially hydrogenated vegetable oil
- Partially hydrogenated saturated fat
- Partially hydrogenated palm oil
- Partially hydrogenated coconut oil
- Hydrogenated soybean oil

Basically, if it says hydrogenated or partially hydrogenated on a food label you should avoid it.

Salt

Salt can increase your blood pressure so keep an eye on how much you are consuming. It may be more than you think!

You can reduce your salt intake by checking out how much is already added to your foods. On food labels it can be listed as sodium and the miniscule amounts may not seem like much but to work out the actual salt content, multiply the sodium amount by 2½. This will tell you how much actual salt the product contains.

Recipes

Healthy Cooking To Lower Your Cholesterol

Before you get started, it's worth going through your cupboards to check food labelling so that you can see what it is you need to avoid. By cooking with fresh whole foods, you'll know exactly what's gone into your food and you'll have weeded out ingredients which offer little or no nutritional benefit.

Now you can begin adding more foods which can actively lower your cholesterol. You might want to start your day with a simple bowl of porridge which is quick and easy to prepare plus increase the amount of fresh fruit, vegetables and fibre you consume.

To stop you reaching for unhealthy snacks, prepare for your day by having handy transportable options in case you get hunger pangs. You can check out the recipes and prepare soups and snacks which are easy to store and delicious.

You can also use cholesterol lowering spreads which contain plant sterols can also be used. The aim of this book is to show you how to eat naturally and healthily without highly processed ingredients. We combine meals with plenty of plant-based protein, vegetables and fruits so that you can reduce your cholesterol naturally. It's thought that although spreads containing plant sterols to lower bad cholesterol, they also lower good cholesterol. The choice is yours, but avoid all trans-fats.

Some of the recipes in the desserts section contain some sugar so these should only be eaten in moderation and preferably once your cholesterol levels are lower.

Wishing you great health and we hope you enjoy the recipes!

BREAKFAST

Muesli

Ingredients

225g (8oz) oats
125g (4oz) mixed dried fruit; raisins, apricots, cranberries or dates
60g (2½ oz) Brazil nuts, chopped
60g (2½ oz) almond flakes
60g (2½ oz) sunflower seeds
2 tablespoons honey
2 tablespoons olive oil
3 tablespoons water
1 teaspoon cinnamon
½ teaspoon ginger

Method

Place the oats, sunflower seeds, almond flakes and nuts into a bowl and mix well. In a separate bowl, combine the oil, honey, cinnamon, ginger and water. Add the oats, seeds and nuts and combine. Scatter the mixture onto a baking tray and bake in the oven at 190C/375F for 30 minutes, until crisp and golden. Remove and allow it to cool. Mix in the dried fruit and store in a container until ready to use. Serve with almond, soya or oat milk.

Cheese & Courgette (Zucchini) Mini Omelettes

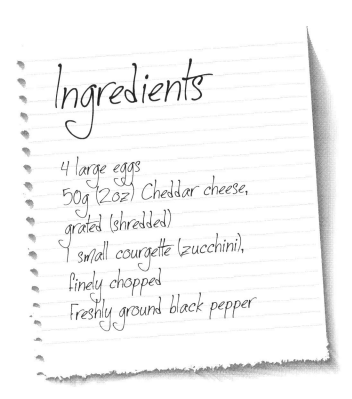

Ingredients

4 large eggs
50g (2oz) Cheddar cheese, grated (shredded)
1 small courgette (zucchini), finely chopped
Freshly ground black pepper

SERVES 4

Method

Whisk the eggs then add the grated cheese and black pepper. Add the courgette (zucchini) and mix well. Lightly grease a muffin tin. Pour in the egg mixture. Bake in the oven at 180C/360F for around 20 minutes until the eggs are set. You can also try other fillings such as spinach, tomatoes, ham, chicken, prawns, mushrooms, spring onions (scallions), olives, peas and feta cheese.

Mexican Omelette

Ingredients

60g (2½ oz) tinned mixed beans, drained
60g (2½ oz) mushrooms, chopped
2 eggs
½ green or red pepper (bell pepper)
1 tablespoon olive oil
Dash of Tabasco sauce or a sprinkle
of chilli powder

SERVES
1

Method

Heat the olive oil in a pan. Add the mushrooms, pepper (bell pepper) and beans. Cook for 3-4 minutes until the vegetables have softened. Remove them and set aside. Whisk the eggs in a bowl and pour them into the pan. Once the eggs begin to set, return the mushrooms, peppers and beans and spread them onto the eggs. Sprinkle with chilli or Tabasco sauce. Serve and eat straight away.

Pear Porridge

Ingredients

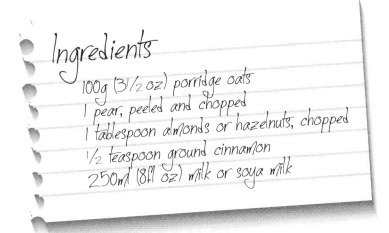

100g (3½ oz) porridge oats
1 pear, peeled and chopped
1 tablespoon almonds or hazelnuts, chopped
½ teaspoon ground cinnamon
250ml (8fl oz) milk or soya milk

SERVES
1

Method

In a saucepan, cook all the ingredients, apart from nuts, for 5 minutes or until it thickens. Serve topped with chopped nuts.

Summer Berry Porridge

Ingredients

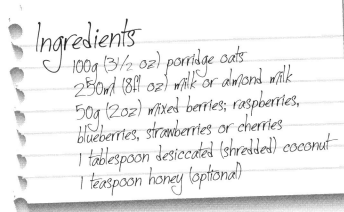

100g (3½ oz) porridge oats
250ml (8fl oz) milk or almond milk
50g (2oz) mixed berries; raspberries, blueberries, strawberries or cherries
1 tablespoon desiccated (shredded) coconut
1 teaspoon honey (optional)

SERVES
1

Method

Place the oats, coconut and milk into a saucepan and cook until the mixture thickens. Serve into a bowl and top it off with berries and a drizzle of honey.

Chicken & Red Pepper Breakfast Pots

SERVES
4

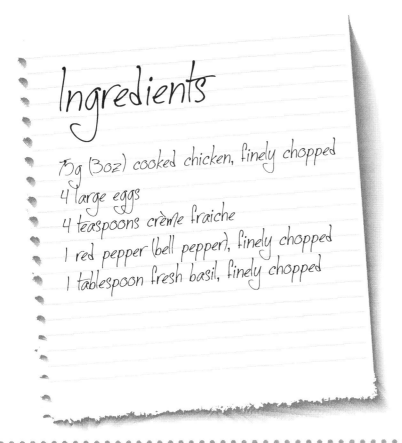

Ingredients

75g (3oz) cooked chicken, finely chopped

4 large eggs

4 teaspoons crème fraiche

1 red pepper (bell pepper), finely chopped

1 tablespoon fresh basil, finely chopped

Method

Lightly grease 4 ramekin dishes then line them with chicken and red pepper (bell pepper) pieces. Crack an egg into each ramekin. Add a teaspoon of crème fraiche and a sprinkle of basil. Place in the oven at 180C/360F for 16 to 18 minutes for soft yolks, longer if you want the eggs completely set. Season and serve.

Fruit & Nut Breakfast Bars

Ingredients

100g (3½ oz) dried apricots
100g (3½ oz) dried figs or dates
100g (3½ oz) dried apple rings, chopped
50g (2oz) cashew nuts, chopped
50g (2oz) sunflower seeds, chopped
100g (3½ oz) rolled oats
2 tablespoons sesame seeds
60mls (2fl oz) fresh apple juice
(not concentrated)
2 tablespoons honey (optional)

MAKES
approx.
24

Method

Grease and line a square baking tray. Place the dried fruit into a blender and process until roughly chopped. Stir in the oats, seeds and nuts and mix well. Add in the apple juice and honey (optional as it may be sweet enough without it) and combine. Spoon the mixture into a baking tray and press it into the sides. Bake in the oven at 190C/375F for 20-25 minutes. Remove from the oven and once it's cooled cut it into bars. These not only make a great on-the-go breakfast but make a delicious snack too.

Almond & Nectarine Yogurt

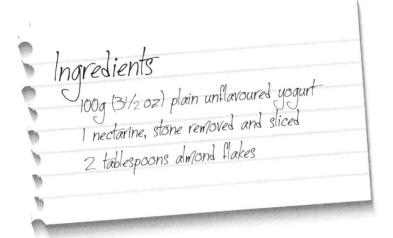

SERVES 1

Ingredients

100g (3½ oz) plain unflavoured yogurt

1 nectarine, stone removed and sliced

2 tablespoons almond flakes

Method

Put half of the nectarine slices into a glass; add a layer of yogurt topped with a sprinkling of almond flakes, followed by another layer of the same. Eat straight away.

Oat Cream Breakfast Bowl

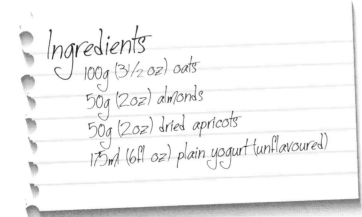

SERVES 1

Ingredients

100g (3½ oz) oats

50g (2oz) almonds

50g (2oz) dried apricots

175ml (6fl oz) plain yogurt (unflavoured)

Method

Make this delicious breakfast the night before by combining all the ingredients in a bowl and chilling it in the fridge until the morning.

Summer Berry Smoothie

Ingredients

1 handful of mixed berries; raspberries, redcurrants, blackberries etc;

1 carrot

1 small orange

SERVES 1

Method

Place all the ingredients into a blender with enough water to cover them and process until smooth.

Spinach & Apple Smoothie

Ingredients

½ carrot

½ apple

½ cucumber

Handful of kale or spinach

1 tablespoon sunflower seeds

1 tablespoon sesame seeds

SERVES 1

Method

Place all the ingredients into a blender and add around a cup of water. Blitz until smooth. You can add a little extra water if it's too thick.

Berry Healthy Smoothie

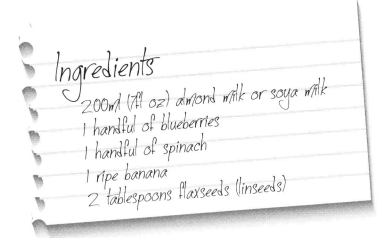

SERVES
1

Ingredients

- 200ml (7fl oz) almond milk or soya milk
- 1 handful of blueberries
- 1 handful of spinach
- 1 ripe banana
- 2 tablespoons flaxseeds (linseeds)

Method

Place all the ingredients into a blender and process until smooth.

Strawberry & Avocado Smoothie

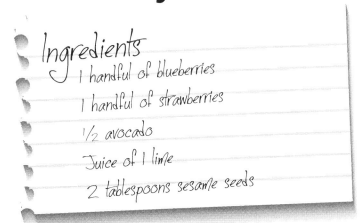

SERVES
1

Ingredients

- 1 handful of blueberries
- 1 handful of strawberries
- ½ avocado
- Juice of 1 lime
- 2 tablespoons sesame seeds

Method

Place all the ingredients into a blender and blitz until smooth.

Blueberry & Oat Smoothie

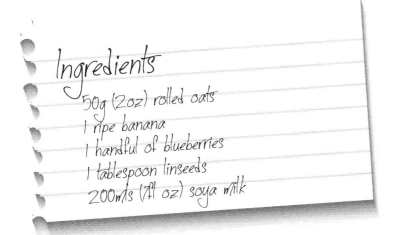

Ingredients

50g (2oz) rolled oats
1 ripe banana
1 handful of blueberries
1 tablespoon linseeds
200mls (7fl oz) soya milk

SERVES
1

Method

Place all the ingredients into a blender and process until smooth.

Minty Strawberry Smoothie

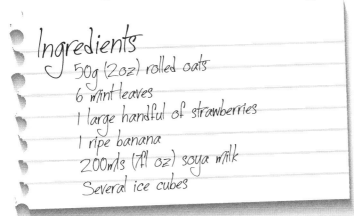

Ingredients

50g (2oz) rolled oats
6 mint leaves
1 large handful of strawberries
1 ripe banana
200mls (7fl oz) soya milk
Several ice cubes

SERVES
1

Method

Place all the ingredients into a blender and blitz. If your blender doesn't process ice you can always crush the ice and add it after blending.

LUNCH

Chicken, Shitake & Barley Soup

Ingredients

SERVES 4

450g (1lb) chicken breasts, chopped
250g (9oz) shitake mushrooms, chopped
75g (3oz) pearl barley
1 carrot, chopped
1 onion, chopped
1 leek, chopped
1 tablespoon fresh parsley, chopped
1 tablespoon fresh thyme, chopped
1 tablespoon butter
1 litre (1 3/4 pints) chicken stock

Method

Place the barley in a saucepan, cover with boiling water and simmer for 5 minutes. Drain the barley and set aside. Heat the butter in a saucepan, add the onion and leek and cook for 4 minutes. Add in the stock (broth) and barley. Bring to the boil, reduce the heat and simmer for 40 minutes. Add the chicken, carrots, mushrooms, parsley and thyme. Cook for around 15-20 minutes until the vegetables have softened. Stir in the parsley and serve.

Minestrone Soup

Ingredients

500g (1lb 2oz) butterbeans, drained and rinsed
25g (1oz) Parmesan cheese, grated (shredded)
4 tomatoes
2 carrots, finely chopped
2 onions, finely chopped
2 cloves of garlic, crushed
1 large courgette (zucchini) finely chopped
1 tablespoon fresh basil leaves, chopped
250g (9oz) passata
750mls (1¼ pints) vegetable stock (broth)
1 tablespoon olive oil

SERVES 4

Method

Place the tomatoes in hot water for a minute or so then remove the skin and seeds and chop it finely. Heat the olive oil in a pan and add the carrots, onions, courgette (zucchini) and garlic. Cook for 3 minutes. Pour in the passata and stock (broth). Bring to the boil, reduce the heat and simmer for 10 minutes. Add in the butterbeans, tomatoes and chopped basil and warm them through. Season with salt and pepper. Serve into bowls and sprinkle with Parmesan.

Avocado & Coriander (Cilantro) Soup

SERVES 4

Ingredients

2 large avocados
900ml (1½ pints) chicken stock (broth)
250ml (½ pint) crème fraiche
2 tablespoons of coriander (cilantro), chopped
Juice of ½ lime

Method

Cut the avocados in half, remove and discard the stone then scoop out the flesh. Place the avocado flesh into a blender. Add 4 tablespoons of the crème fraiche and blitz until smooth. In a saucepan, heat the chicken stock (broth) and add the remaining crème fraiche. Add the lime juice to the avocado mixture and mix. Gently stir in the avocado mixture to the chicken stock, keeping it on a low heat until it's combined. Add the coriander (cilantro), season and serve.

Lentil & Sweet Potato Soup

Ingredients

450g (1lb) sweet potatoes, peeled and diced

200g (7oz) red lentils

4 large tomatoes, skinned, de-seeded & chopped

1 carrot, chopped

1 large onion, chopped

1 red pepper (bell pepper), chopped

1 clove garlic, chopped

1 tablespoon olive oil

2 tablespoons fresh basil, chopped

1 litre (1 3/4 pints) stock (broth)

SERVES 4

Method

Heat the olive oil in a saucepan, add the onion and garlic and cook for 4 minutes. Add in the sweet potatoes, carrots, lentils, tomatoes and red pepper (bell pepper) then pour in the stock (broth). Bring to the boil, reduce the heat and simmer for 30 minutes or until the vegetables are soft. Allow to cool for 10 minutes then using a hand blender or food processor blend slightly but leave the soup chunky. Add in the fresh basil leaves and heat further if required before serving.

Tomato & Basil Soup

Ingredients

6 large tomatoes, peeled and chopped
1 onion, finely chopped
4 tablespoons fresh basil, chopped
3 tablespoons olive oil
900mls (1½) pints vegetable stock (broth)
Freshly ground black pepper

SERVES
4

Method

Heat the oil in a saucepan and add the onion. Cook for 5 minutes until it softens. Add in the tomatoes and simmer gently until the tomatoes are soft and pulpy. Add the stock (broth) and cook for 5 minutes. Season with pepper and add 3 tablespoons of fresh basil. Blend in a liquidiser or use a hand blender and process until smooth. Stir in the remaining basil just before serving.

Miso Soup

Ingredients

225g (8oz) pak choi (bok choy), chopped
200g (7oz) tofu, cubed
10 spring onions (scallions), finely chopped
3 tablespoons red miso
1 tablespoon fresh coriander (cilantro), chopped
1 cm (½ inch) chunk of fresh ginger root,
very finely chopped
1 small red chilli
1 star anise
2 tablespoons soy sauce (low sodium)
1200mls (2 pints) vegetable stock (broth)

SERVES 4

Method

Place the pak choi (bok choy), ginger, star anise, chilli and vegetable stock (broth) into a saucepan. Bring to the boil, reduce the heat and simmer for 10 minutes. Add the spring onions (scallions), tofu and soy sauce. Cook for 4 minutes. In a bowl, mix together the red miso with a few tablespoons of the soup then stir the miso into the soup. Stir in the coriander (cilantro) and serve.

Broccoli & Chive Soup

Ingredients

1 head of broccoli, broken into florets
1 onion, chopped
3 tablespoons crème fraiche
2 tablespoons olive oil
600mls (1 pint) vegetable stock (broth)
Squeeze of lemon juice
Large handful of chives, chopped
Freshly ground black pepper

SERVES
4

Method

Heat the oil in a saucepan, add the onion and cook until softened. Add the broccoli and vegetable stock (broth). Bring to the boil, reduce the heat and simmer for 20 minutes. Stir in most of the chopped chives, just hold a few back for garnish. Using a hand blender or food processor blitz the soup until smooth. Stir in the crème fraiche and lemon juice. Season with pepper. Serve into bowls and garnish with chives.

Pear & Celeriac Soup

Ingredients

2 pears, cored, peeled and chopped
1 celeriac, peeled and chopped
1 onion, chopped
2 tablespoons fresh chives, chopped
2.5cm (1 inch) chunk fresh root ginger
600ml (1 pint) vegetable stock (broth)
2 tablespoons olive oil
Freshly ground black pepper

SERVES 4-6

Method

Heat the olive oil in a saucepan, add the onion, celeriac, pears, ginger and cook for 5 minutes. Pour in the vegetable stock (broth) bring to the boil, reduce the heat and simmer for 20-25 minutes. Using a hand blender or food processor, blend the soup until it's smooth. You can add extra stock (broth) or hot water to make the soup thinner if you wish. Sprinkle in the chives. Season with pepper then serve into bowls.

Chicken & Vegetable Soup

Ingredients

225g (8oz) chicken, cut into small cubes
2 stalks of asparagus, chopped
1 courgette (zucchini), finely chopped
1 carrot, chopped
1 stick of celery, chopped
900mls (1½ pints) chicken stock (broth)
½ teaspoon lemon juice
1 tablespoons olive oil
Freshly ground black pepper

SERVES 4

Method

Heat the olive oil in a frying pan. Add the chicken and cook for 10 minutes. Place the chicken, stock (broth) and lemon juice into a large saucepan. Cook for 5 minutes. Add the courgette (zucchini), carrot, celery and asparagus. Continue cooking for around 20 minutes, until the vegetables are soft. Season the soup with and pepper. Serve and eat immediately.

Turkey & Lentil Soup

Ingredients

400g (14oz) cooked turkey, leftovers are great
75g (3oz) cauliflower florets
200g (7oz) mushrooms, chopped
200g (7oz) red lentils
1 onion, chopped
1 courgette (zucchini) chopped
1 carrot, chopped
1 red pepper (Bell pepper), chopped
1 clove of garlic
1200mls (2 pints) chicken stock (broth)
1 tablespoon olive oil

SERVES 4

Method

Heat the olive oil in a saucepan, add the onion and garlic and cook for 4 minutes. Stir in the red pepper (bell pepper), cauliflower, carrot, lentils and mushrooms. Pour in the stock (broth). Bring to the boil, reduce the heat and simmer for 20 minutes. Add in the courgette (zucchini) and turkey. Cook for another 5-10 minutes. Serve and enjoy

Crab & Corn Soup

Ingredients

450g (1lb) sweetcorn
225g (8oz) crabmeat
4 spring onions (scallions) chopped
1cm (½ inch) chunk fresh ginger, chopped
2 teaspoons cornflour
1 egg white
2 tablespoons fresh coriander (cilantro) chopped
1200mls (2 pints) chicken stock (broth)
1 tablespoon Chinese rice wine
3 tablespoons soy sauce (low sodium)

SERVES 4

Method

Place the stock (broth), crab meat and sweetcorn into a wok or saucepan, bring to the boil and simmer for 15 minutes. Stir in the ginger, spring onions (scallions) rice wine and soy sauce. Simmer for 5 minutes. In a small bowl or cup, mix the cornflour with a tablespoon or two of cold water. Pour the mixture into the soup and stir until the soup thickens slightly. In a bowl, whisk the egg white then pour it into the soup while constantly stirring. Sprinkle in the coriander (cilantro). Serve into bowls.

Smoked Fish Chowder

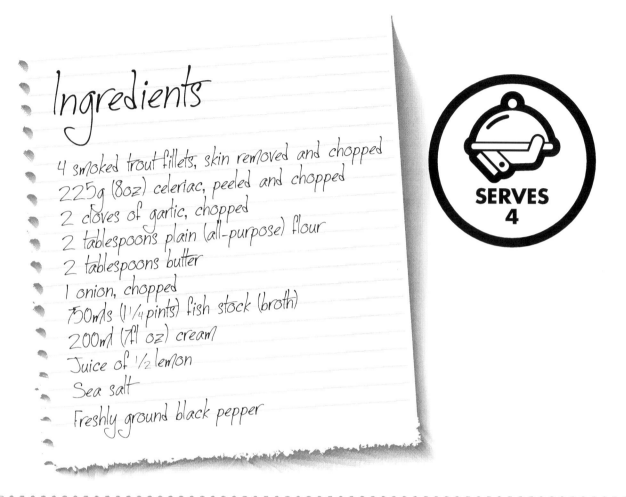

Ingredients

4 smoked trout fillets, skin removed and chopped
225g (8oz) celeriac, peeled and chopped
2 cloves of garlic, chopped
2 tablespoons plain (all-purpose) flour
2 tablespoons butter
1 onion, chopped
750mls (1¼ pints) fish stock (broth)
200ml (7fl oz) cream
Juice of ½ lemon
Sea salt
Freshly ground black pepper

SERVES 4

Method

Heat the butter in a frying pan and add the garlic, onion and celeriac. Cook for around 4 minutes. Stir in the flour and add the fish stock (broth). Add in half the trout and the cream. Simmer for around 20 minutes. Using a hand blender or food processor blitz the soup until smooth. Add in the lemon juice and season with salt and pepper. Add in the remaining pieces of fish and heat if necessary. Serve into bowls.

Mackerel & Bean Salad

Ingredients

400g (14oz) trimmed green beans
2 smoked mackerel fillets, skin removed
1 tin of drained butterbeans
1 small bunch of spring onions (scallions),
chopped
Lemon juice
Freshly ground black pepper

SERVES
2

Method

Slice the green beans and steam them for 5 minutes, or until they soften but maintain their crunch. Mix the green beans in a bowl with the butterbeans and add the chopped spring onions. Chop the 2 mackerel fillets into small pieces and mix it all together. Season with pepper and lemon juice before serving.

Avocado & Orange Salad

Ingredients

2 large avocados, peeled, stone removed
3 oranges, peeled
2 teaspoons cardamom pods
Large handful of watercress
2 tablespoons olive oil
1/2 teaspoon ground allspice
Juice of 1/2 lime

SERVES 4

Method

Cut the orange flesh from the outer skin to remove the individual segments and place them in a bowl. Slice the avocados and add them to the orange segments. Using the back of a spoon or a mortar and pestle, break the cardamom pods open and remove the tiny seeds. In a bowl, mix together the cardamom seeds with the lime juice, olive oil and allspice. Toss the oranges, avocados and watercress in the dressing then serve.

Mackerel & Dill Pate

Ingredients

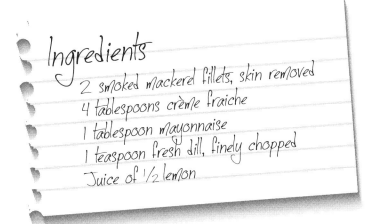

2 smoked mackerel fillets, skin removed
4 tablespoons crème fraiche
1 tablespoon mayonnaise
1 teaspoon fresh dill, finely chopped
Juice of 1/2 lemon

SERVES
2

Method

Place the mackerel fillets in a bowl and mash them with a fork. Add the crème fraiche, mayonnaise, dill and mix together. Stir in the lemon juice. Spoon the pate into individual ramekin dishes. Chill before serving.

Tuna & Haricot Bean Salad

Ingredients

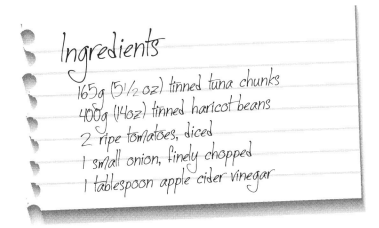

165g (5½ oz) tinned tuna chunks
400g (14oz) tinned haricot beans
2 ripe tomatoes, diced
1 small onion, finely chopped
1 tablespoon apple cider vinegar

SERVES
2

Method

Combine all of the ingredients in a bowl and serve.

Tomato & Aubergine (Eggplant) Gratin

Ingredients

50g (2oz) Cheddar cheese, grated (shredded)
4 large ripe tomatoes
2 ripe aubergines (eggplants)
2-3 tablespoons olive oil

SERVES 4-6

Method

Cut the tomatoes into slices and set aside. Thinly slice the aubergines (eggplants) and place them under a hot grill (broiler). Brush with olive oil and cook for 15 minutes turning once. Place the tomato slices and aubergine slices in an oven-proof dish, alternating between slices of each. Cover with the grated cheese. Transfer to the oven and bake at 200C/400F for 15 minutes, or until the cheese is golden. Serve and eat immediately.

Aubergine (Eggplant) Dip & Pitta Bread

Ingredients

4 brown wholemeal pitta breads
2 aubergines (eggplants)
2 tablespoons fresh parsley
1 garlic clove, peeled
1 tablespoon lemon juice
1/2 teaspoon cumin

SERVES 4

Method

Cut the stalk off the top of the aubergines (eggplants). Place the whole aubergines on a griddle pan with the garlic and cook for around 15 minutes. Remove them and set aside to cool. Scoop out the aubergine flesh and transfer it to a food processor along with the garlic, parsley, lemon juice and cumin. Blitz until smooth. Slice the pitta breads and warm them under a grill for 5 minutes. Serve the aubergine dip with the pitta bread and a green salad.

Sushi Rolls

Ingredients

8 nori sheets

150g (5 oz) grated carrots

150g (5oz) red pepper, finely chopped

150g (5oz) cucumber, finely chopped

150g (5oz) alfalfa sprouts

150g (5oz) brown rice

1 ripe avocado, chopped

2 teaspoons fresh dill or chives, chopped

Tahini or hummus

SERVES 4

Method

Lay out the nori sheets (shiny side down). Spread the tahini or hummus onto the nori sheets. Make a row of rice in the middle of the nori sheet. Add carrots, red pepper, cucumber, alfalfa and avocado. Leave one inch of the nori sheet uncovered to seal the sushi roll. Top with a sprinkling of dill or chives. Tightly roll the nori sheet from the bottom to make a firm sushi roll. Cut into 2cm (1 inch) pieces and serve. For a variation, try spreading the sushi with guacamole instead of hummus.

Chicken Pittas & Coleslaw

Ingredients

½ red cabbage, finely chopped
2 large chicken breasts, cooked and sliced
3 tablespoons crème fraiche
1 onion, finely chopped
1 apple, peeled, cored and chopped
1 tablespoon lemon juice
4 large brown pitta bread pockets
Freshly ground black pepper

SERVES 2

Method

Place the cabbage in a bowl and combine it with the onion, apple, crème fraiche and lemon juice. Season with pepper. Stir in the chicken breast making sure it's coated in the dressing. Warm the pitta pockets under a grill and make an incision along the side. Fill the pittas with the coleslaw and chicken mixture. Serve and enjoy.

Mushroom & Red Wine Pâté

Ingredients

350g (12oz) mushrooms
150ml (5fl oz) red wine
2 onions, finely chopped
1 clove garlic, chopped
1/2 teaspoon dried mixed herbs
2 tablespoons fromage frais
1 tablespoon olive oil

SERVES
4

Method

Heat the oil in a saucepan, add the garlic and onion and cook for 5 minutes until softened. Stir in the mushrooms and cook for 4 minutes. Pour in the red wine and add the herbs. Bring to the boil, reduce the heat and simmer until the liquid has been absorbed. Remove from the heat and allow to cool. Once the mushroom mixture is completely cold stir in the fromage frais. Transfer the pate to a serving bowl and serve.

Turkey Burgers & Salsa

Ingredients

450g (1lb) turkey mince
50g (2oz) fine oats
1 clove garlic
1 teaspoon chive
1 tablespoon Dijon mustard
1 egg
1 handful of rocket (arugula) leaves
Dash of Tabasco sauce (optional)
1-2 tablespoons olive oil
Wholemeal burger buns

SERVES 4

Method

Place all of the ingredients, except the burger buns, into a bowl and using your hands mix everything together. Shape the mixture into patties. Heat the olive oil in a frying pan, add the patties and cook for around 5 minutes on either side until cooked through. Put a few rocket (arugula) leaves into the burger buns, add the turkey burgers and top if off with some salsa (see page 109).

Sweet Potato & Spinach Bites

Ingredients

- 450g (1lb) sweet potatoes, peeled and chopped
- 125g (4oz) spinach leaves
- 4 tablespoons plain (all-purpose) flour
- 3 spring onions (scallions)
- 2-3 tablespoons sesame seeds
- 2 tablespoons fresh coriander (cilantro) leaves
- Olive oil for frying

SERVES 4

Method

Boil the sweet potato for around 20 minutes until it's tender then drain them. Mash the potatoes and set aside. Dip the spinach in boiling water for around a minute until it has wilted. Drain the excess moisture off the spinach then combine it with the mashed sweet potato. Add the spring onion (scallions), coriander (cilantro) and combine. Form the mixture into small patties. Roll the patties in sesame seeds and flour. Heat the oil in a large frying pan. Carefully add the patties to the oil and cook them for around 3-4 minutes until they are crisp and golden. Serve with salsa or dips.

Five-Spice Pork Salad

Ingredients

4 boneless pork steaks, cut into strips
175g (6oz) lettuce, chopped
100g (3½ oz) mange tout (snow peas), sliced
2 stalks of celery, finely chopped
½ cucumber, finely chopped
1 green pepper (bell pepper) chopped
3 teaspoons Chinese five-spice
3 tablespoons fish sauce
3 tablespoons rice vinegar
2 tablespoons sesame oil
2 tablespoons olive oil
2cm (1 inch) chunk fresh ginger, grated (shredded)
2 tablespoons fresh coriander (cilantro) chopped

SERVES 4

Method

Place the olive oil, fish sauce, five-spice, ginger and vinegar together in a bowl and mix well. Add the pork strips, coat them in the marinade then cover and chill for 1 hour, or longer if you can. Heat the sesame oil in a frying pan or wok. Add the pork and marinade and cook for 3-4 minutes or until cooked through. Combine the lettuce, celery, cucumber, mange tout (snow peas) in a bowl. Add in the cooked pork strips and the marinade juices. Serve with rice or noodles and eat immediately.

Quick Chicken Casserole

Ingredients

4 chicken breasts

3 carrots, chopped

2 parsnips, chopped

½ turnip, peeled and chopped

600ml (1 pint) gravy, ready-mixed or home-made

3 tablespoons olive oil

Freshly ground black pepper

SERVES 4

Method

Heat the oil in a large saucepan. Add the chicken and cook for 5 minutes. Add in the carrots, parsnip and turnip. Cook for around 15 minutes then add in the gravy and cook for 10 minutes. Season with pepper before serving.

Mediterranean Baked Cod

Ingredients

650g (1lb 7oz) new potatoes, roughly sliced
450g (1lb) cherry tomatoes
100g (3½ oz) pitted black olives
4 cod fillets
1 onion, roughly chopped
Small handful of fresh basil leaves
150ml (5fl oz) vegetable stock (broth)
3 tablespoons olive oil
Juice of 1 lemon

SERVES 4

Method

Place the sliced potatoes and onion into an oven-proof dish. Pour in the vegetable stock (broth) and bake in the oven at 180C/350F for 15 minutes. Remove from the oven and add the cod, tomatoes, olives, lemon juice and olive oil. Return it to the oven and cook for around 15 minutes or until the cod is cooked through. Add extra olive oil or water if necessary. Sprinkle with basil and serve.

Salmon Kebabs

Ingredients

12 cherry tomatoes
9 pitted black olives
4 salmon fillets
4 tablespoons fresh parsley
1 tablespoon olive oil
Rind and juice of a lemon

SERVES
4

Method

Cut the salmon into 4cm (1½ inch) chunks. Place them in a bowl along with just half of the parsley, lemon rind and juice. Cover and allow to marinate for at least 30 minutes. Thread the salmon chunks onto skewers and alternate them with tomatoes and olives. Place the kebabs under a hot grill (broiler) for 10-12 minutes or until the salmon is thoroughly cooked. In a separate bowl mix together the remaining lemon juice, rind and parsley with a tablespoon of olive oil. Serve the kebabs and spoon over the lemon/oil dressing. Serve with rice and green salad.

Pork & Mushroom Cream Sauce

SERVES 4

Ingredients

6 large mushrooms, sliced

4 boneless pork chops

2 medium shallots, finely chopped

180ml (6fl oz) double cream (heavy cream)

2 tablespoons olive oil

Sea salt

Freshly ground black pepper

Method

Heat the oil in a large frying pan over a medium-high heat. Add the chops reduce the heat and fry for 3 or 4 minutes per side, or until cooked through. Transfer the chops to a plate and cover with foil to keep them warm. Reduce the heat of the frying pan and add the mushrooms and shallots to the pan. Cook until softened. Pour in the cream and season with salt and pepper. Stir until warmed through. Serve the pork chops with the pepper sauce. It goes really well with mashed celeriac on the side.

Parmesan Pumpkin

Ingredients

1.6kg (3½ lb) pumpkin, peeled, de-seeded and sliced
50g (2oz) breadcrumbs
50g (2oz) parmesan cheese, grated (shredded)
2 eggs, whisked
2 tablespoons fresh basil leaves
1 onion, finely chopped
1 clove garlic, chopped
400ml (14fl oz) passata
4 tablespoons olive oil

SERVES 6

Method

Heat the oil in a saucepan, add the garlic and onion and cook for 5 minutes. Stir in the passata and herbs. Simmer for 10 minutes. Whisk the eggs in a bowl and place the breadcrumbs onto a plate. Dunk the slices of pumpkin into the egg and then dip them in the breadcrumbs. Heat the oil in a frying pan and cook the pumpkin until golden. Transfer them to an ovenproof dish, cover with passata and sprinkle with Parmesan. Bake in the oven at 180C/350F for around 20 minutes.

Prawn Pasta

Ingredients

350g (12oz) fusilli whole-wheat pasta
350g (12oz) prawns, peeled and cooked
200g (7oz) peas
200ml (7fl oz) stock (broth)
1 small onion, chopped
2 tablespoons fresh parsley, chopped
1 tablespoon olive oil
Small pinch of saffron

SERVES
4

Method

Heat the oil in a saucepan, add the onion and cook for 5 minutes until soft. Stir in the peas and prawns and cook for 3 minutes. Cook the pasta according to the instructions. In the meantime, pour the stock (broth) and saffron into the frying pan. Cook until the liquid has reduced to approximately half. Add in the cooked pasta, Sprinkle with parsley. Season if required. Serve and enjoy.

Spicy Edamame (Soy Beans)

Ingredients

400g (14oz) edamame (soy beans), frozen or fresh

400g (14oz) tinned chopped tomatoes

4 shallots, chopped

2 teaspoons grated root ginger

2 teaspoons garam masala

1 tablespoon olive oil

Method

Heat the olive oil in a frying pan, add the shallots and cook for 3 minutes. Stir in the ginger and garam masala then add the chopped tomatoes. Cook for 4 minutes. Add the edamame and heat them thoroughly. Serve with salad or as a delicious accompaniment to chicken, fish and meat.

Sardines, Egg & Tomato

Ingredients

24 fresh sardines, filleted
4 tomatoes, skins removed and finely chopped
4 tablespoons plain (all-purpose) flour
2 eggs, hard-boiled
7 tablespoons olive oil
Freshly ground black pepper
1 tablespoon fresh parsley

SERVES 4

Method

Dredge the sardines in the flour and set aside. Heat 2 tablespoons of olive oil in a frying pan and cook the sardines for 3-4 minutes until golden. Season with pepper. Peel and finely chop the eggs. Place the eggs in a bowl and add in the remaining olive oil and mix with the tomatoes, parsley and pepper. Divide the sardines onto plates with the eggs and tomatoes spooned on top. Serve alongside green salad.

Almond Crusted Chicken

Ingredients

75g (3oz) ground almonds (almond meal)
4 chicken breasts

1 egg
1/4 teaspoon sea salt
1/4 teaspoon white pepper
1/2 teaspoon paprika
4 tablespoons olive oil

SERVES
4

Method

Place the ground almonds into a bowl with the paprika, salt and pepper and mix well.
In a separate bowl, beat the egg. Dip the chicken breasts into the egg, then dredge it
in the almond mixture. Heat the olive oil in a frying pan and add the chicken. Cook for
about 5-6 minutes on each side until the chicken is golden and cooked thoroughly.

Salmon & Dill Burgers

Ingredients

600g (1½lb) salmon fillets, skin removed
50g (2oz) fresh dill
1 garlic clove
1 egg
1 spring onion (scallion) finely chopped

SERVES 4-6

Method

Place the salmon in a food processor with the spring onion (scallion), dill and garlic. Blend it until smooth. Place the mixture in a medium bowl and combine with the egg. Using your hands, shape the mixture into patties. Place the burgers under a grill for 15 minutes, turning once halfway through.

Chilli Bean Bake

Ingredients

- 2 x 400g (2 x 14oz) tins of chopped tomatoes
- 400g (14oz) haricot beans
- 125g (5oz) rolled oats
- 50g (2oz) Cheddar cheese, grated (shredded)
- 100g (3½ oz) peas
- 3 handfuls of spinach leaves
- 2 cloves garlic, crushed
- 1 onion, chopped
- 4 tablespoons olive oil
- 1 tablespoon soy sauce (low sodium)
- 1 teaspoon chilli flakes
- 1 teaspoon dried oregano

SERVES 4

Method

Heat the olive oil in a frying pan, add the garlic, onion, chilli and oregano. Cook for 5 minutes. Add in the chopped tomatoes, oats and beans and cook for 5 minutes. Stir in the peas, spinach and soy sauce. Transfer the mixture to an ovenproof dish and sprinkle with cheese. Bake in the oven at 200C/400F for 10 minutes until the cheese is bubbling.

Asparagus, Cashew & Beansprouts

Ingredients

225g (8oz) asparagus
150g (5oz) mange tout (snow peas)
150g (5oz) bean sprouts
6 spring onions (scallions) chopped
3 tablespoons cashew nuts
2 tablespoons grated ginger root
2 tablespoons sesame oil
2 garlic cloves, chopped
3 tablespoons soy sauce (low sodium)

SERVES 4

Method

Heat the oil in a frying pan or wok. Add the garlic, ginger, spring onions (scallions) and asparagus. Cook for 3-4 minutes, stirring constantly. Stir in the mange tout (snow peas) and cook for 3 minutes. Add in the cashews, bean sprouts and soy sauce and warm them for a minute or so. Serve with rice.

Fast Chicken Curry

Ingredients

4 chicken breasts, cubed
3 tablespoons mild curry powder
1 onion, chopped
1 teaspoon ground coriander (cilantro)
1 bay leaf
1 teaspoon ground ginger
600mls (1 pint) chicken stock (broth)
2 tablespoons olive oil

**SERVES
4**

Method

Heat the oil in a frying pan, add the onion and cook until it softens. Add the coriander (cilantro), curry powder, ginger and the bay leaf and cook for 5 minutes. Add the chicken and chicken stock (broth). Cook for 15 minutes or until the chicken is cooked thoroughly. Remove the bay leaf and serve with brown rice.

Smokey Bean & Mushroom Stew

Ingredients

400g (14oz) black-eyed peas
400g (14oz) haricot beans
400g (14oz) tinned tomatoes, chopped
225g (8oz) chestnut mushrooms, sliced
150g (5oz) sweetcorn
2 garlic cloves, chopped
2 onions, chopped
1 tablespoon smoked paprika
1 red chilli, finely chopped
1 large handful of parsley
250ml (8fl oz) vegetable stock (broth)
1 tablespoon soy sauce (low sodium)
1 tablespoon olive oil

SERVES 4

Method

Heat the oil in a saucepan, add the onions and garlic and cook for 4 minutes until the onions have softened. Stir in the mushrooms, chilli, haricot beans, black-eyed peas, sweetcorn, tomatoes, paprika and soy sauce and cook for 5 minutes. Pour in the stock (broth) and simmer for 15 minutes. Stir in the parsley and serve into bowls.

Fresh Salmon & Rice Salad

Ingredients

400g (14oz) brown basmati rice

4 salmon fillets

1 cucumber, diced

1 large bunch of spring onions (scallions), finely chopped

1 large handful of coriander (cilantro) leaves, finely chopped

1 tablespoon soy sauce (low sodium)

Juice of ½ lemon

SERVES
2

Method

Boil the rice according to the instructions then set aside. Grill the salmon fillets for around 15 minutes until cooked through, turning once half way through. Remove the salmon skin and flake the salmon through the rice. Combine the rice mixture with the cucumber, spring onions (scallions), coriander (cilantro), lemon juice and soy sauce. Serve and enjoy.

Speedy Vegetable Curry

Ingredients

300g (11oz) frozen mixed vegetables
400g (14oz) tinned chopped tomatoes
2 clove garlic, chopped
2 tablespoons tomato puree (paste)
2-3 tablespoons curry powder
1 large onion, chopped
360ml (12fl oz) vegetable stock (broth)
2 tablespoons olive oil
1 small handful coriander (cilantro) chopped

**SERVES
4**

Method

Heat the oil in a saucepan. Add the onion and garlic and cook until softened. Stir in the tomato puree (paste) and curry powder and cook for 2 minutes. Add in the vegetables, tomatoes, stock (broth). Cook for around 20 minutes, or until the vegetables are cooked through. Stir in the coriander (cilantro) leaves and serve with brown rice or a baked potato.

DINNER

Chicken Stir-Fry

Ingredients

600g (1lb 5oz) cooked brown rice
4 chicken breasts, cut into strips
1 courgette, finely chopped
2 red peppers (bell peppers) sliced
4 spring onions (scallions), finely chopped
1 carrots, very finely chopped
1 red onion, finely chopped
2 cloves garlic, chopped
2cm (1 inch) chunk fresh ginger, finely chopped
1-2 groundnut oil
2 teaspoons cornflour (cornstarch)
2 tablespoons soy sauce (low sodium)
120ml (4fl oz) chicken stock (broth)
Freshly ground black pepper

SERVES 4

Method

Heat the oil in a frying pan or wok then add the ginger and garlic. Cook for 1 minute. Add in the chicken and fry for around 4 minutes until golden. Remove and set aside. Place the vegetables into the pan and cook for 3-4 minutes. In a bowl, combine the cornflour and soy sauce. Return the chicken to the pan and stir in the cooked rice. Heat thoroughly. Pour in the stock (broth) add the cornflour mixture and stir until slightly thickened. Season with pepper.

Oat Crusted Herring & Salsa

Ingredients

4 herring fillets
50g (2oz) rolled oats
2 tablespoons milk
2 teaspoons Dijon mustard

For the salsa
1 red pepper (bell pepper) de-seeded
and finely chopped
4 tomatoes, finely chopped
2 spring onions (scallions), finely chopped
Squeeze of lemon juice

SERVES
4

Method

Place the tomatoes, red pepper (bell pepper), spring onions (scallions) and lemon juice into a bowl and mix together. Set aside. In a separate bowl, mix together the mustard and milk. In another bowl place the oats. Dip the fish in the mustard mixture then dredge in the oats. Place the herring on a baking sheet and bake in the oven at 200C/400F for 20 minutes. Serve alongside the salsa.

Creole Chicken

Ingredients

4 chicken breasts
250g (9 oz) mangetout (snow peas)
2 x 400g (14oz) tinned chopped tomatoes
4 cloves garlic, chopped
1 tablespoons curry powder
1 teaspoon ground cumin
1/2 teaspoon paprika
200mls (7fl oz) chicken stock (broth)
3 tablespoons olive oil

SERVES 4

Method

Heat the oil in a frying pan, add the chicken, cumin, paprika and curry powder and cook until the chicken is browned. Add the garlic, tomatoes and stock. Bring to the boil then reduce the heat and simmer for 25 minutes. Stir in the mangetout (snow peas) and cook for 10 minutes. Serve with brown rice.

Lamb Shanks & Lentils

Ingredients

2 lamb shanks

300g (11oz) puy lentils

3 carrots, chopped

3 cloves of garlic, crushed

1 onion, finely chopped

2 tablespoons tomato puree (paste)

2 bay leaves

1 bouquet garni

750ml (1¼ pints) beef or vegetable stock (broth)

3 tablespoons olive oil

SERVES 2

Method

Place the oil in a saucepan, place it on a hob at a high heat. Add the lamb, turning occasionally until it is brown all over. Transfer the lamb to a bowl and set aside. Add the onion, carrots and garlic to the saucepan and cook for 5 minutes. Return the lamb to the saucepan and add in the stock, tomato puree (paste), bouquet garni, bay leaves and lentils. Transfer to an oven-proof dish, cover and cook in the oven at 200C/400F for 2 hours. Check half way through cooking and add extra stock (broth) or water if necessary. Serve and enjoy.

Fish Pie

Ingredients

700g (1lb 9oz) filleted white fish, cod or haddock
200g (7oz) prawns, peeled and cooked
700g (1lb 9oz) cooked potatoes, mashed
25g (1oz) cornflour
4 tablespoons fresh parsley, chopped
2 bay leaves
1 small onion, roughly chopped
1 sprig of thyme
1 teaspoon lemon zest
600mls (1 pint) soya milk

SERVES 6

Method

Place the soya milk in a saucepan with the onion, bay leaves, thyme and lemon zest. Add the fish and bring to the boil. Gently simmer for 15 minutes until the fish is cooked through. Strain the milk off the fish and set aside, ready to make the sauce. Discard the onion, bay leaves, thyme and zest. Flake the fish into chunks and place in an oven-proof casserole dish. To make the sauce, mix the cornflour with a splash of milk to make a paste. Stir the paste into the milk you set aside. Place it on the heat and stir until it thickens. Add in the parsley and prawns. Stir and cook for 2 minutes. Pour the sauce over the fish. Top it off with mashed potatoes. Transfer the fish pie to the oven and cook for 30 minutes at 180C/350F until the mashed potato is slightly golden.

Roast Autumn Vegetables

Ingredients

250g (9oz) peas, fresh or frozen

150g (5oz) button mushrooms

3 tablespoons toasted seed mix; sesame seeds, pumpkin seeds or flaxseeds

2 whole beetroot, unpeeled

2 cloves of garlic

1 butternut squash, peeled and cut into chunks

1 head of broccoli

2 tablespoons olive oil or ground nut oil

Freshly ground black pepper

SERVES
4

Method

Wash the beetroot then place it on a baking tray and sprinkle with salt. Place it in the oven at 200C/400F for around 1 hour or until tender. Place the squash on a separate baking tray and coat it with a little olive oil then transfer it to the oven and bake for around 45 minutes or until tender. In the meantime, steam the broccoli and peas for 5 minutes. Once the roast vegetables are cooked, heat the olive oil in a frying pan and add the garlic and mushrooms. Cook for around 3 minutes. Chop the beetroot and squash chunks and combine with the other vegetables. Sprinkle with seeds, season with black pepper and serve.

Beef Satay

Ingredients

450g (1lb) rump steak or sirloin steak, sliced
6-8 tablespoons smooth peanut butter
3 teaspoons curry powder
400ml (14fl oz) coconut milk
2 teaspoon soy sauce (low sodium)
Juice of ½ lemon
Dash of Tabasco sauce

**SERVES
4**

Method

In a bowl, combine the peanut butter and coconut milk. Stir in the curry powder, Tabasco and soy sauce. Thoroughly coat the beef pieces in the peanut mixture. Thread the beef onto skewers, and set aside the remaining satay sauce. Place the beef skewers under a hot grill (broiler) and cook for 4-5 minutes on each side, making sure they are thoroughly cooked. Pour the remaining satay sauce into a small saucepan and the lemon juice and bring to the boil. Serve the chicken skewers and pour the remaining satay sauce on top.

Chickpea & Vegetable Casserole

Ingredients

1 x 400g (14oz) chopped tinned tomatoes
1 x 400g (14oz) tinned chickpeas (garbanzo beans) rinsed and drained
3 large carrots, chopped
3 cloves of garlic, chopped
2 stalks celery, finely chopped
2 tablespoons freshly chopped parsley
1 bouquet garni
1 onion, finely chopped
1 courgette (zucchini), chopped
9 00ml (1½ pints) vegetable stock
4 tablespoons olive oil

SERVES 4

Method

Heat the oil in a saucepan and add the onion and garlic. Cook gently for 5 minutes. Add in the carrots, celery and tinned tomatoes. Cook for another 5 minutes. Add the chickpeas (garbanzo beans), courgette, bouquet garni and stock (broth) to the saucepan. Simmer for 15 minutes. Remove the bouquet garni. Sprinkle in the parsley and serve with baked potatoes.

Chicken Chilli

Ingredients

2 x 400g (2 x 14oz) tin of chopped tomatoes
300g (11oz) tin of kidney beans
4 chicken breasts, sliced
2 teaspoons chilli power
2 teaspoons cumin
1 red pepper (bell pepper), finely chopped
1 large onion, finely chopped
600mls (1 pint chicken stock (broth)
1 tablespoon olive oil

SERVES 4-6

Method

Warm the oil in a frying pan, add the onion and cook until soft. Stir in the chilli and cumin. Add the tomatoes and stock (broth) and bring to the boil. Stir in the red pepper (bell pepper) and sliced chicken breasts. Cover the saucepan, reduce the heat and simmer for around 15 minutes. Add in the kidney beans and simmer for 20 minutes.

As a serving option, instead of rice, you can go for the low carb option by spooning the chicken chilli into firm lettuce leaves such as iceberg or romaine lettuce. Add guacamole and cheese, for a really delicious yet light meal.

Aubergine and Feta Towers

Ingredients

150g (5oz) feta cheese, chopped
8 tomatoes, finely chopped
4 tablespoons pine nuts
2 aubergines (eggplants)
2 tablespoons olive oil
1 handful of basil leaves, chopped

For the tomato sauce

1 x 400g (14oz) tin of tomatoes
1 red chilli
2 tablespoons olive oil

SERVES
4

Method

Cut the aubergines (eggplants) into slices around 2.5cm (1 inch) thick. Heat 2 tablespoons of oil in a pan, add the aubergine and cook for 3 minutes on either side. Remove and set aside. In a bowl, combine the tomatoes, feta cheese and basil. Dry fry the pine nuts for 1 minute until lightly toasted and mix them with the tomatoes and feta. On a baking sheet, place the 4 largest slices of aubergine and add a spoonful of the tomato, cheese and basil mixture. Select the next largest pieces, place on top, followed by more tomato mixture. Continue stacking like this until you have 4 slices of aubergine piled up with the tomato mixture in between. Bake in the oven at 180/360F for 12 minutes. For the tomato sauce, place the tomatoes, chilli and olive oil into a blender and blitz until smooth then heat the sauce. Serve the aubergine towers and spoon the tomato sauce onto the side.

Chicken & Avocado Salad

Ingredients

300g (10oz) black-eyed peas
4 skinless cooked chicken breasts, chopped
1 cucumber, peeled, deseeded and chopped
2 avocados, de-stoned and flesh scooped out
2 tablespoons olive oil
12 Little Gem lettuce leaves
2 teaspoons mixed seeds (sunflower, sesame or flaxseed)
Splash of Tabasco sauce
Juice of ½ lemon

SERVES 4

Method

Rinse the black-eyed peas in cold water and drain. Put the chicken, black-eyed peas and cucumber into a bowl. Place the avocados, Tabasco, lemon juice and olive oil in a food processor and blitz until smooth. Combine the avocado mixture with the chicken and black-eyed peas. Spoon the mixture into the lettuce leaves. Sprinkle with the seeds. Chill and serve.

Falafels

Ingredients

400g (14oz) tin of chickpeas (garbanzo beans)
75g (3oz) mushrooms, chopped
50g (2oz) breadcrumbs
2 cloves garlic, chopped
2 spring onions (scallions) chopped
1 egg
1 small handful of parsley, chopped
1 small handful of coriander (cilantro) leaves, chopped
1 tablespoon curry powder
1 teaspoon ground cumin
4 tablespoons olive oil

SERVES 4

Method

Heat a tablespoon of olive oil in a frying pan and add the mushrooms and spring onions (scallions). Cook for 2 minutes. Place the chickpeas (garbanzo beans) in a food processor along with the garlic and blitz until smooth. Transfer the mixture to a bowl and combine it with the onions, mushrooms, breadcrumbs, egg, herbs and spices. Shape the falafel mixture into patties. Heat 3 tablespoons of olive oil in the frying pan. Place the falafels into the pan and cook for around 5 minutes or until golden. Serve with salads or use in place of a beef burger.

Swordfish With Lemon & Basil

SERVES 4

Ingredients

4 swordfish steaks
4 tablespoons basil leaves, chopped
4 tablespoons olive oil
2 cloves of garlic
Juice of 1 lemon
Freshly ground black pepper

Method

Mix together the lemon juice, olive oil, garlic and basil and season with pepper. Place the fish on a plate and lightly coat the swordfish with 1-2 tablespoons of the lemon oil mixture. Heat a little olive oil in a hot pan and add the swordfish steaks. Cook for 3-4 minutes on each side and check that it's completely cooked. Serve onto plates with the remaining dressing.

Turkey Burgers With Tomato & Pepper Salsa

Ingredients

450g (1lb) turkey mince
4 spring onions (scallions)
3 cloves garlic, crushed
2 teaspoons cumin
2 teaspoons ground coriander
1 egg
1/2 teaspoon chilli flakes
Freshly ground black pepper

SERVES
4

Method

Combine all of the ingredients in a bowl then allow them to chill in the fridge for 30 minutes. Using clean hands, shape the mixture into 8 patties then place them under a hot grill (broiler) for 6 minutes on each side or until cooked through. Serve with tomato and pepper salsa (see recipe on page 109).

Lamb Casserole

Ingredients

- 450g (1lb) lamb steaks, cubed
- 16 pitted dates
- 4 tablespoons fresh parsley, chopped
- 3 carrots, roughly chopped
- 2 onions, roughly chopped
- 2 garlic cloves, chopped
- 1 tablespoon plain (all-purpose) flour
- 1 tablespoon tomato puree (paste)
- 2 tablespoons olive oil
- 600ml (1 pint) lamb, chicken or beef stock (broth)

SERVES 4

Method

Coat the lamb in the flour. Heat the oil in a frying pan, add the lamb and brown it for 10 minutes. Add in the garlic, carrots and onions and cook for 5 minutes. Pour in the stock (broth) and cook for 20 minutes. Stir in the dates, tomato puree (paste) and parsley. Season if required. Serve with brown rice, quinoa or couscous.

Feta, Almond & Quinoa Salad

Ingredients

350g (12oz) quinoa
125g (4oz) feta cheese
60g (2½ oz) almond flakes
1 teaspoon ground coriander (cilantro)
1 teaspoon turmeric
1 handful of coriander (cilantro) leaves, chopped
Juice of 1 lime
600mls (1 pint) hot water
1-2 tablespoons olive oil
Freshly ground black pepper

SERVES 4

Method

Heat the olive oil in a large frying pan, add the ground coriander and turmeric and stir. Add in the quinoa and mix it with the spices. Pour in the hot water, stir and simmer for around 12 minutes or until the quinoa grains have opened out. Remove from the heat. Stir in the feta cheese, almond flakes, coriander (cilantro) leaves and lime juice. Season with salt and pepper. This dish can be eaten straight away or chilled before serving.

Turkey & Spring Vegetable Casserole

Ingredients

675g (1½lb) new potatoes
225g (8oz) carrots, chopped
225g (8oz) asparagus, chopped
200g (7oz) sugar-snap pears
4 turkey steaks
1 large onion, chopped
1 bay leaf
1 handful of tarragon, chopped
300ml (½ pint) chicken stock (broth)
175ml (6fl oz) crème fraiche
4 tablespoons olive oil

SERVES 4

Method

Heat the olive oil in a pan, add the turkey and onion and cook for around 5 minutes. Stir in the carrots, potatoes and cook for 3 minutes. Pour in the stock (broth) and add the bay leaf. Cook for 20 minutes or until the potatoes are soft. Add the asparagus and sugar-snap peas and cook for 4 minutes. Stir in the crème fraiche and tarragon. Remove the bay leaf and serve.

Herby Chicken Goujons

Ingredients

450g (1lb) chicken mini-fillets
(or breast cut into strips)
100g (3 1/2 oz) finely milled oats
1 teaspoon fresh thyme, chopped
1 teaspoon paprika
2 tablespoons olive oil

SERVES
4

Method

Place the oats, thyme and paprika into a food processor and blitz until finely ground, then place the oats onto a plate. Coat the chicken with a little olive oil, and then dredge them in the oat mixture. Grease a baking sheet with olive oil and lay the chicken onto it. Bake in the oven at 220C/425F for 15-20 minutes, or until the chicken is cooked through and golden.

Sea Bass & Green Vegetables

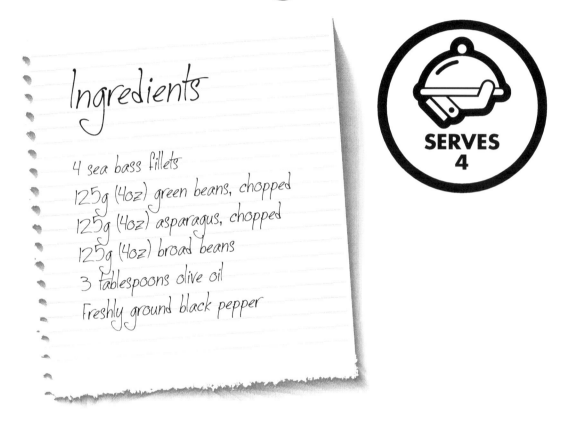

SERVES 4

Ingredients

4 sea bass fillets
125g (4oz) green beans, chopped
125g (4oz) asparagus, chopped
125g (4oz) broad beans
3 tablespoons olive oil
Freshly ground black pepper

Method

Heat the olive oil in a pan then add the fish fillets and fry them for around 3 minutes on each side. Meanwhile place the green beans, asparagus and broad beans into a steamer and cook for 5 minutes until cooked through but crisp. Season with pepper and serve them onto a plate and add the fish on top of the vegetables. Enjoy.

Chicken & Vegetable Bake

Ingredients

225g (8oz) new potatoes, chopped
20 cherry tomatoes
20 pitted black olives
8 chicken thighs
2 stalks of celery, roughly chopped
1 aubergine (eggplant), cut into chunks
1 red pepper (bell pepper), de-seeded and chopped
1 onion, roughly chopped
1 teaspoon mixed herbs
1 teaspoon paprika
3 tablespoons olive oil
Juice of ½ lemon
Handful of fresh basil leaves

SERVES 4

Method

Place the olive oil, paprika and lemon juice into a bowl and stir. Place the potatoes and vegetables, except for the olives and tomatoes, into a large oven-proof dish and pour around half of the paprika oil mixture over them. Add the chicken thighs on top of the vegetables and drizzle the paprika oil over the chicken. Sprinkle in the dried herbs. Cover the dish with foil and bake in the oven at 200C/400F for 30 minutes. Remove the foil from the dish, add the tomatoes and olives and cook for another 15 minutes. Check the chicken is cooked through and the vegetables are soft. Sprinkle with basil leaves and serve.

Chickpea & Tomato Spaghetti

Ingredients

350g (12oz) spaghetti

2 x 400g (14oz) tins of chickpeas (garbanzo beans)

175g (6oz) spinach leaves

50g (2oz) Parmesan cheese, grated (shredded)

For the sauce:

400g (14oz) tinned chopped tomatoes

1 stalk of celery, finely chopped

1 red onion, finely chopped

2 cloves garlic, chopped

2 tablespoons olive oil

1/2 teaspoon Tabasco sauce

SERVES 4

Method

Heat the olive oil in a saucepan and add the onion, Tabasco sauce, celery and garlic. Cook for around 4 minutes. Pour in the chopped tomatoes, bring to the boil then reduce the heat and simmer for around 15 minutes. Stir in the chickpeas (garbanzo beans) and spinach. Allow to cook for 2 minutes. In the meantime, cook the spaghetti according to the instructions. When cooked, toss the spaghetti in the sauce. Serve with a sprinkling of Parmesan cheese.

Balsamic Spiced Roast Vegetables

Ingredients

- 4 cloves garlic, chopped
- 2 aubergines (eggplants), sliced
- 1 butternut squash, peeled de-seeded and chopped
- 1 red pepper (bell pepper), sliced
- 1 green pepper (bell pepper), sliced
- 1 yellow pepper (bell pepper) sliced
- 1 onion, chopped
- 1 teaspoon ground coriander (cilantro)
- 1 teaspoon ground cumin
- 1 handful of fresh basil or marjoram, chopped
- 2 tablespoons balsamic vinegar
- 2 tablespoons olive oil

SERVES 4

Method

Place all of the vegetables into a roasting tin and sprinkle in the cumin, coriander (cilantro), olive oil and balsamic vinegar. Apart from the fresh herbs, toss everything together and make sure it's well coated. Roast in the oven at 220C/425F for 25-30 minutes or until the vegetables have softened and are caramelised. Stir in the fresh herbs. Serve with a green leafy salad. As an alternative the vegetables can be topped with grated cheese.

Chinese Style Quinoa Salad

Ingredients

300g (11oz) quinoa
150g (5oz) sweetcorn
150g (5oz) peas
5 radishes, chopped
1 large carrot, grated (shredded)
1/2 cucumber, diced
1 red pepper (bell pepper) chopped
Handful of sultanas
Handful of cashew nuts

For the dressing:
1cm (1/2inch) chunk of fresh ginger, grated (shredded)
1/2-1 teaspoon chilli flakes (or according to taste)
3 tablespoons soy sauce (low sodium)
1 tablespoon sesame oil
1 tablespoon olive oil

SERVES
4

Method

Boil the quinoa for around 12 minutes or until the grains have opened and are soft then drain it. Combine all of the vegetables, sultanas and nuts in a large bowl and stir in the quinoa. In separate bowl mix together the ingredients for the dressing. Pour the dressing onto the salad and mix well. Can be eaten hot or cold.

DESSERTS, TREATS & SNACKS

Berry & Almond Crumble

Ingredients

350g (12oz) raspberries
350g (12oz) blueberries
300g (11oz) ground almonds
100g (3½oz) coconut oil
50g (2oz) desiccated (shredded) coconut
2 tablespoons honey
Zest of 1 lemon

SERVES
2

Method

Place the ground almonds, coconut and lemon zest into a bowl and mix together. Warm the honey and coconut oil and pour into the almond mixture and combine. Put the raspberries and blueberries into an oven-proof dish. Cover them with the almond and coconut mixture. Bake in the oven at 180C/350F for 15 minutes until the top becomes slightly golden. Serve with crème fraiche or yogurt.

Creamy Stuffed Peaches

Ingredients

4 large ripe peaches, halved and stone removed
100g (3½oz) cream cheese
2 tablespoons oat bran
1 tablespoon honey
Zest of 1 orange

SERVES
4

Method

Place the peaches in an oven-proof dish with the flat side facing up. Place the orange zest, oat bran, cream cheese and honey into a bowl and combine the ingredients. Spoon the creamy mixture into the centre of the peaches. Bake them in the oven at 180C/360F for 15 minutes. Serve them on their own or with a little crème fraiche or plain yogurt.

Banana Biscuits

Ingredients

2 ripe bananas
50g (2oz) butter, melted
50g (2oz) oats
50g (2oz) ground almonds
25g (1oz) ground linseeds (flaxseeds)
Vanilla extract or vanilla pod

MAKES approx. 20

Method

Mash up the bananas in a large bowl and mix with the melted butter and vanilla. Add all of the remaining ingredients and combine. Leave to stand for 10 minutes and the mixture will firm up. Use a teaspoon to scoop out the dough. Roll it into balls and then pat down on a lined baking tray. Bake at 180C/360F for 15-20 minutes or until golden brown.

Banana Chocolate Bites

Ingredients

4 teaspoons cocoa powder
4 teaspoons desiccated (shredded) coconut
2 bananas, sliced diagonally

SERVES 2

Method

Put the cocoa powder and coconut on separate plates. Roll each banana slice in the cocoa, shake off the excess and dip into the coconut. Set on a plate and eat immediately.

Chocolate & Hazelnut Clusters

MAKES 24

Ingredients

125g (4oz) dark chocolate
(min 70% cocoa)
125g (4oz) dates, chopped
50g (2oz) hazelnuts, chopped

Method

Place the chocolate into a bowl and place the bowl over a saucepan of simmering water. Once the chocolate has melted, remove it from the heat. Stir in the hazelnuts and dates. Spoon the mixture into small paper cases and allow it to set. Alternatively, you can use almonds, Brazils, cashews, apricots or sultanas.

Baked Apples

Ingredients

4 large Bramley apples
50g (2oz) raisins
2 tablespoons honey
1/4 teaspoon cinnamon
Knob of butter

SERVES
4

Method

Core the apples, leaving a small piece at the bottom to retain the filling. Place the raisins inside the apple and pour a little honey and cinnamon into the centre of each one. Place the apples in the oven and bake at 180C/360F for 35 minutes. Serve with crème fraiche or a little yogurt with a sprinkling of cinnamon or nutmeg.

Apple Soufflé Omelette

Ingredients

2 eggs
1 large sweet apple, peeled, cored
and chopped
1 teaspoon butter
Sprinkling of cinnamon

SERVES
1

Method

Heat the apple with 2-3 tablespoons of water, until it becomes soft and pulpy. Stir in the cinnamon and set it aside. Separate the egg yolks from the whites and whisk the whites into soft peaks. Beat the yolks then fold them into the mixture.

Heat the butter in a small frying pan and pour in the eggs. Cook the omelette until the eggs have set but are light and fluffy. Transfer to a plate, spoon on the apple and fold it over. Enjoy.

Brazil Nut Brittle

Ingredients

150g (5oz) Brazil nuts, chopped
150g (5oz) dark chocolate
(min 70% cocoa)

SERVES
4-6

Method

Place the chocolate in a bowl and place it over a saucepan of gently simmering water and let it melt. In the meantime, place half of the chopped Brazil nuts in the bottom of a small dish or small loaf tin. When the chocolate has melted and is smooth, pour half of it over the chopped nuts. Add in the remaining chopped nuts and pour over the remaining melted chocolate. Chill in the fridge until it hardens. Break the brittle into chunks and serve.

Flapjacks

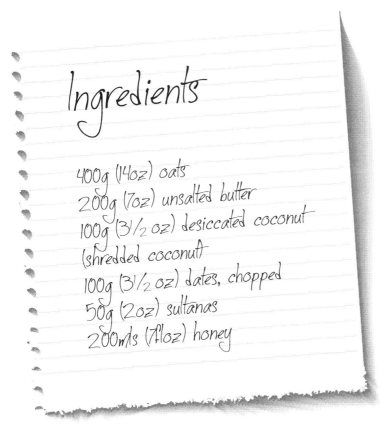

Ingredients

400g (14oz) oats
200g (7oz) unsalted butter
100g (3½ oz) desiccated coconut
(shredded coconut)
100g (3½ oz) dates, chopped
50g (2oz) sultanas
200mls (7floz) honey

MAKES approx. 16

Method

Place the butter in a saucepan and gently warm it. Stir in the honey, sultanas and dates and cook until soft. Add in the coconut and the oats and combine all the ingredients. Line a baking tin with parchment paper and transfer the mixture to the tin. Press it down well. Bake the mixture in the oven at 180C/360F for 20 minutes. Remove the baking tin from the oven and cut into squares but don't take them out. Allow it to cool completely before removing the flapjacks.

Chocolate Mendiants

Ingredients

150g (5oz) dark chocolate
(min 70% cocoa)
50g (2oz) dried apricots, chopped
50g (2oz) sultanas or cranberries
50g (2oz) blanched almonds
25g (1oz) pistachio nuts

MAKES
12

Method

Line 2 or 3 baking sheets with parchment paper. Place the chocolate in a bowl and place the bowl over a saucepan of gently simmering water. Once the chocolate has melted, remove it from the heat. Spoon the chocolate into circular shapes measuring around 5-6cm (2½ inches). Sprinkle each disc with equal amounts of the fruit and nuts. Let the chocolate cool until it's set.

Raspberry & Pistachio Fool

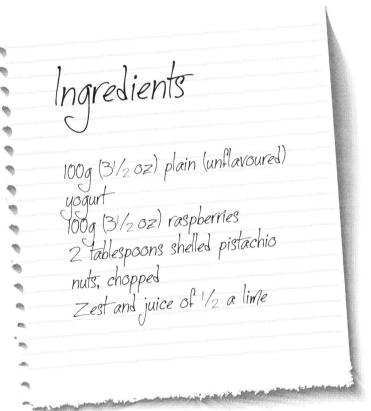

Ingredients

100g (3½ oz) plain (unflavoured) yogurt
100g (3½ oz) raspberries
2 tablespoons shelled pistachio nuts, chopped
Zest and juice of ½ a lime

**SERVES
2**

Method

Place the raspberries into a blender and puree until smooth. Place the yogurt, lime zest and juice into the raspberry puree. Stir but don't mix it completely, aim for a swirled affect. Spoon the yogurt and raspberry mixture into 2 serving glasses or bowls. Top it with the pistachio nuts and serve.

Sultana & Pear Loaf

Ingredients

125g (4oz) self-raising flour
125g (4oz) sultanas
25g (1oz) oats
2 pears, cored, peeled and grated (shredded)
50g (2oz) brown sugar
2 tablespoons apple juice
2 tablespoons olive oil
½ teaspoon bicarbonate of soda (baking soda)
2 teaspoons mixed spice
1 egg

**SERVES
6-8**

Method

Grease and line a 450g (1lb) loaf tin with parchment paper. Place the oats in a bowl and combine them with the grated pears, brown sugar, apple juice and olive oil. Stir in the sultanas, flour, mixed spice, egg and bicarbonate of soda (baking soda). Mix it all thoroughly. Transfer the mixture to the lined loaf tin. Bake in the oven at 180C/360F for 55-60 minutes. Insert a skewer and if it comes out clean you can remove it from the oven. Remove the loaf from the tin and rest it on a wire rack to cool.

Strawberry & Chocolate Frozen Yogurt

SERVES 8

Ingredients

225g (8oz) strawberries
1200mls (2 pints) plain yogurt, (unflavoured)
2 tablespoons 100% cocoa powder
Strawberries to garnish

Method

Place the strawberries into a food processor along with half of the yogurt and process until smooth and creamy. Combine the remaining yogurt with the cocoa powder and mix it really well. Line a small loaf tin with grease-proof paper or plastic wrap. Spread ½ the strawberry yogurt mixture into the loaf tin and smooth it out. Next add all of the chocolate yogurt mixture. Spoon on the remaining strawberry yogurt so you have alternating layers of strawberry and chocolate. Freeze for 3 hours or longer. Place a serving plate over the tin and gently tip out the frozen dessert. Remove the wrap. Garnish with a few fresh strawberries, slice and serve.

CONDIMENTS

Walnut & Mint Pesto

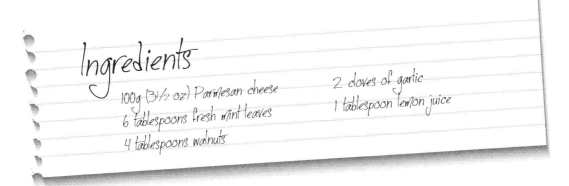

Ingredients

100g (3½ oz) Parmesan cheese
6 tablespoons fresh mint leaves
4 tablespoons walnuts

2 cloves of garlic
1 tablespoon lemon juice

Method

Put all the ingredients into a food processor and blend until it becomes a smooth paste.

Chive & Broad Bean Dip

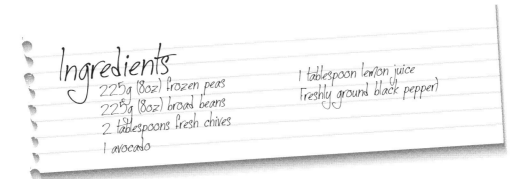

Ingredients

225g (8oz) frozen peas
225g (8oz) broad beans
2 tablespoons fresh chives
1 avocado

1 tablespoon lemon juice
Freshly ground black pepper)

Method

Boil the peas and beans in water until warmed through then drain them and allow them to cool. Place all of the ingredients into a blender and process until smooth. Transfer the dip to a bowl and chill before serving. It's delicious served as a dip for crudités.

Tomato & Red Pepper Salsa

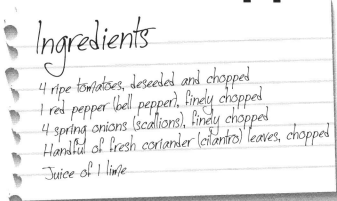

Ingredients

4 ripe tomatoes, deseeded and chopped
1 red pepper (bell pepper), finely chopped
4 spring onions (scallions), finely chopped
Handful of fresh coriander (cilantro) leaves, chopped
Juice of 1 lime

Method

Place the red pepper (bell pepper) under a hot grill (broiler) and cook until the skin blisters. Place the pepper in a bowl and cover with plastic wrap for 2 minutes to loosen the skin then peel it. Discard the skin and chop the flesh. Combine the pepper in a bowl with the chopped tomatoes, coriander (cilantro) and spring onions (scallions). Add the juice of the lime and serve.

Basil & Pumpkin Seed Pesto

Ingredients

100g (3½ oz) fresh basil leaves
50g (2oz) pumpkin seeds
1 clove garlic
3 tablespoons olive oil

Method

Place all the ingredients into a blender and process. Add extra olive oil if you prefer it thinner.

Cucumber Raita

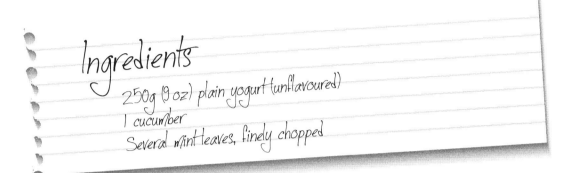

Ingredients
250g (9 oz) plain yogurt (unflavoured)
1 cucumber
Several mint leaves, finely chopped

Method

Grate the cucumber then wrap it in a clean tea towel to eliminate excess water. Place the cucumber in a bowl and stir in the yogurt and chopped mint. Chill before serving with hot curries or as a refreshing dip.

Cashew Salsa

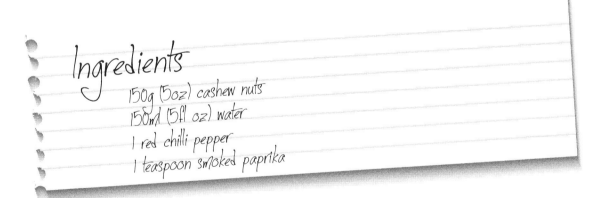

Ingredients
150g (5oz) cashew nuts
150ml (5fl oz) water
1 red chilli pepper
1 teaspoon smoked paprika

Method

Dry fry the cashew nuts in a frying pan until golden brown then allow them to cool. Place all of the ingredients into a blender and process until smooth. Serve with crudités or tortilla chips.

Watercress Salsa

Ingredients

75g (3oz) fresh watercress
3 tablespoons fresh basil leaves
1 clove garlic
2 tablespoons olive oil
2 tablespoons lemon juice

Method

Place all the ingredients into a blender and process until smooth.
Serve as an accompaniment to fish.

Edamame Dip

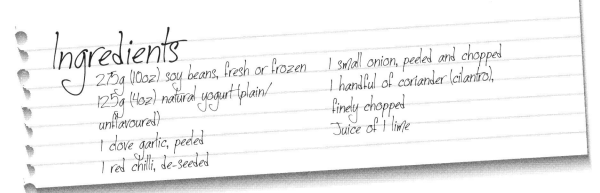

Ingredients

275g (10oz) soy beans, fresh or frozen
125g (4oz) natural yogurt (plain/
unflavoured)
1 clove garlic, peeled
1 red chilli, de-seeded

1 small onion, peeled and chopped
1 handful of coriander (cilantro),
finely chopped
Juice of 1 lime

Method

Cook the soya beans for 4-5 minutes then rinse them in cold water until cool. Transfer the soya beans to a food processor and add the yogurt, garlic, chilli, onion and lime juice. Process until smooth. Stir in the coriander (cilantro). Serve with crudités.

Tomato Vinaigrette

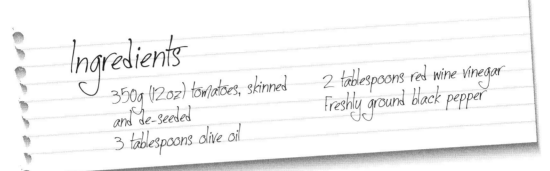

Ingredients

350g (12oz) tomatoes, skinned and de-seeded

3 tablespoons olive oil

2 tablespoons red wine vinegar

Freshly ground black pepper

Method

Place the ingredients into a blender and blitz until smooth. Season if required. Serve as an accompaniment to salad and meat dishes.

Basil & Caper Relish

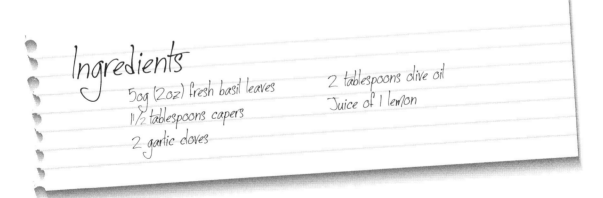

Ingredients

50g (2oz) fresh basil leaves

1½ tablespoons capers

2 garlic cloves

2 tablespoons olive oil

Juice of 1 lemon

Method

Place all the ingredients into a blender and blitz until smooth.

20091260R00068

Printed in Poland
by Amazon Fulfillment
Poland Sp. z o.o., Wrocław